Lynxes

by Barbara Keevil Parker and Duane F. Parker

Lerner Publications Company • Minneapolis

To Natalya, Jessica, Logan

Our thanks to Colleen Sexton for her editorial expertise

Note: *There are several kinds of lynxes, including the Eurasian lynx (pictured on cover), the Spanish lynx, and the North American lynx (also known as the Canada lynx). This book focuses on the North American lynx.*

The photographs in this book are used with the permission of: © Tom Brakefield/SuperStock, pp. 4, 14, 31; © Tom and Patty Leeson, pp. 6, 8, 10, 11, 18, 19, 22, 24, 26, 27, 29, 33, 34, 40, 43; Photodisc Royalty Free by Getty Images, pp. 7, 36; © SuperStock, Inc./SuperStock, pp. 9, 13; © Alan G. Nelson/Root Resources, pp. 12, 17, 21; © Michele Burgess, p. 15; © W. Perry Conway/CORBIS, pp. 16, 25, 30; © Galen Rowell/CORBIS, p. 20; © Erwin and Peggy Bauer, p. 23; © Joe McDonald/Visuals Unlimited, pp. 28, 32; © Jim Brandenburg/Minden Pictures, p. 35; © Kenneth W. Fink/Root Resources, p. 37; © Photocyclops.com/SuperStock, 38; © Gary Neil Corbett/SuperStock, p. 39; © Darrell Gulin/CORBIS, p. 41; © age fotostock/ SuperStock, pp. 42, 46–47.
Cover image: © Royalty-Free/Corbis.

Lerner Publications Company
A division of Lerner Publishing Group
241 First Avenue North
Minneapolis, MN 55401   U.S.A.

Website address: www.lernerbooks.com

Library of Congress Cataloging-in-Publication Data

Parker, Barbara Keevil.
    Lynxes / by Barbara Keevil Parker and Duane F. Parker.
      p. cm. — (Early bird nature books)
    Includes index.
    ISBN-13: 978–0–8225–2871–5 (lib. bdg. : alk. paper)
    ISBN-10: 0–8225–2871–1 (lib. bdg. : alk. paper)
    1. Lynx—Juvenile literature. I. Parker, Duane F. (Duane Frank), 1937– II. Title. III. Series.
QL737.C23P3543 2006
599.75'3—dc22   2004028803

Manufactured in the United States of America
1 2 3 4 5 6 – JR – 11 10 09 08 07 06

Contents

The North American lynx lives in Canada and the United States. The striped areas show exactly where North American lynxes live.

Be a Word Detective

Can you find these words as you read about the lynx? Be a detective and try to figure out what they mean. You can turn to the glossary on page 46 for help.

carnivore	**kittens**	**retracts**
den	**nurse**	**ruff**
habitat	**predator**	**tufts**
home range	**prey**	

Chapter 1

This animal is a lynx. How is a lynx different from a house cat?

Lynxes Are Cats

A small wildcat peeks through the low branches of an evergreen tree. This wildcat looks like a house cat. But it is much bigger.

The wildcat has long fur around its face. Spiky black hairs stand up from the tips of its ears. This wildcat is a North American lynx.

The lynx belongs to the cat family. The cat family has big cats, such as tigers and lions. All big cats can roar. It has small cats, such as cougars and bobcats. Small cats can't roar.

The bobcat is a close relative of the lynx.

The North American lynx is a small cat. A male lynx weighs about 25 pounds. A female lynx weighs a little less. A lynx is about 2 feet tall and 3 feet long.

The scientific name of the North American lynx is Lynx canadensis.

You can tell that it is winter by the gray coat on this lynx.

A lynx's fur is short and thick. Its winter coat is smoky gray. The lynx's fur turns red brown in the summer. The fur on its belly and the insides of its legs is light colored. Fur keeps the lynx warm in cold weather. It keeps rain and snow away from the lynx's skin.

Notice the black hair on the lynx's ears and tail.

Some of a lynx's fur is black. The lynx has tufts of black fur at the tips of its ears. The tufts look like paintbushes dipped in black paint. The lynx's short tail has a black tip.

A ruff of fur forms a collar around the lynx's neck. Sometimes the ruff makes the lynx look like it is wearing a bow tie. The ruff helps keep the lynx warm.

The fur on a lynx's neck looks sort of like a bow tie.

A lynx has strong legs. They help the lynx run fast. The lynx's back legs are longer than its front legs. The long back legs help the lynx jump.

A lynx has long, strong back legs that make the lynx good at jumping.

A lynx's large paws are good for walking on snow.

A lynx has large furry feet. The bottom of a lynx's foot looks like a baseball catcher's mitt. Thick fur grows around and between the footpads. The lynx's feet spread out when it walks. Its feet act like snowshoes. They keep the lynx from sinking into deep snow.

Chapter 2

This lynx lives in North America. Where else do lynxes live?

Lynx Homes

A habitat (HAB-uh-tat) is the natural home where an animal lives. The North American lynx lives mainly in Canada and Alaska. Other kinds of lynxes live on the other side of the world. The Eurasian lynx makes its home in the forests of eastern Europe and Asia. The Spanish lynx lives only in Spain.

A North American lynx looks for a home far away from people. It lives in thick forests. The lynx roams the forest's rock ledges, brush, and swampy ground. The forest is cold in winter. The snow is deep. But the lynx knows how to survive in harsh weather.

The winters are long and snowy where the lynx lives in North America.

Each lynx chooses a home range. A home range is the area where a lynx lives, hunts, and raises its young. The lynx marks its home range. It sprays urine on bushes and trees at the edges of its home range. It leaves droppings. Scratching trees is another way the lynx might mark its home range. All of these markings tell other lynxes to stay away.

A lynx raises its young in its home range.

A lynx strolls through its home range.

Home ranges are different sizes. A lynx's home range is small when there is plenty of food. A lynx needs to travel farther when food is hard to find. Then its home range is bigger.

Chapter 3

This lynx is hunting for food. What does a lynx eat?

The Hunter

Like other cats, the lynx is a carnivore (KAHR-nuh-vor). Carnivores eat meat. The lynx is also a predator (PREH-duh-tur). Predators hunt other animals for food. Animals that are hunted for food are prey.

The North American lynx's favorite prey is the snowshoe hare. The lynx also eats red squirrels, birds, mice, voles, and other small animals.

A lynx must be quick to catch a snowshoe hare.

A lynx sleeps during the day. It wakes up at night to hunt. The lynx needs to kill one small animal every few days to survive. The snowshoe hare makes up most of a lynx's diet. That means a lynx must kill about 150 to 200 snowshoe hares each year.

A lynx usually hunts at night.

Hares are lynxes' main food.

The number of lynxes grows when there are a lot of hares to hunt. But sometimes there are too many hares. They eat all the plants in an area. The hares run out of food. With no food, hares die. Then lynxes do not have enough to eat. With no food, lynxes die. The number of hares and lynxes goes up and down over time.

Lynxes are excellent jumpers.

The lynx is a good hunter. It chases its prey. A lynx can run about 30 miles per hour for short distances. The lynx can jump as far as 15 feet. It can also jump 8 feet into the air. That is almost as high as a basketball hoop. Jumping helps the lynx catch its prey.

A lynx uses the sharp claws on its feet to hunt. It scratches a tree or log to sharpen its claws. When the lynx is not using its claws, it retracts them. The lynx pulls its claws into its paws. Retracting the claws helps them stay sharp.

Lynxes keep their claws retracted in their paws when they are not using them.

A lynx's eyes and ears are important for hunting. The lynx's eyes are much stronger than people's eyes. The lynx might be able to see a snowshoe hare from 1,000 feet away. This distance is about the length of three football fields. The lynx also sees better in the dark than other cats.

Lynxes have very good eyesight.

A lynx sneaks up on its prey.

A lynx's ears can hear higher and fainter sounds than people's ears do. The tuft of hair on the end of each ear acts like a radio antenna. The tufts pick up very soft sounds. The lynx listens for the sound of its prey moving. Then it creeps toward the sound. The lynx gets ready, then springs on the animal. The lynx bites the prey to kill it. Then the lynx begins to eat.

Chapter 4

Baby lynxes are called kittens. What time of year are lynx kittens born?

Lynx Families

A female lynx searches for a den when she is ready to give birth. She looks for a hollow log, a rocky ledge, or a tangle of brush. She wants her den to be a safe and dry place to raise her kittens. The female lynx makes the den soft. She lines it with hairs and evergreen needles.

Most lynx kittens are born in May or June. A mother lynx usually has four to five kittens. But she may have only two or three kittens when food is scarce. The mother lynx raises her kittens alone. The father lynx does not help.

A mother lynx raises her kittens by herself.

Lynx kittens are helpless when they are born. Kittens weigh about 7 ounces at birth. That's about the weight of a can of tuna fish. One kitten could fit inside a cereal bowl.

Newborn kittens are small and helpless. But they grow fast.

A mother lynx cleans her kitten.

The mother lynx stays close to her kittens to keep them warm. She purrs and mews. She uses her nose to push the kittens toward her belly. Each kitten finds a nipple on her belly. They begin to nurse. Nursing is drinking mother's milk.

This young kitten still has blue eyes.

A kitten's eyes are closed at birth. The
kitten opens its eyes when it is about two weeks
old. The kitten's eyes are bright blue. But they
will change to yellow after a few months.

The kittens begin to explore their den on wobbly legs. They also play-fight with each other. Playing helps them learn how to hunt. Soon the kittens pounce on anything that moves.

Kittens learn to hunt by playing with each other.

The kittens stay near the den. They sleep or play when their mother goes hunting. The mother lynx starts bringing the kittens meat when they are one month old. They eat the meat. But their mother's milk is still their main food.

The kittens stay close to home while their mother goes hunting.

As the kittens get older, they follow their mother on short hunting trips.

The kittens follow their mother on short trips when they are six weeks old. But they cannot hunt yet. They feed on animals their mother kills.

These young lynxes are old enough to hunt for their own food.

The mother lynx teaches her kittens how to catch prey. The kittens start to hunt when they are six to eight months old. Sometimes the mother and kittens hunt as a family. Sometimes a kitten hunts alone. The kittens practice. They get better and better at catching their own prey.

Young lynxes leave their mother when they are about nine months old. The young lynxes stay together for a few months. Then they each find their own home range. A wild lynx lives for about 10 to 15 years.

These lynxes will soon be old enough to find their own home ranges.

Chapter 5

Lynxes hunt hares and other small animals. What animals hunt lynxes?

People and the Lynx

The North American lynx has enemies in the wild. Wolves and cougars hunt lynxes. But people are the biggest threat to the lynx.

Fur traders began hunting lynxes 200 years ago. People liked the lynx's soft, thick fur. They made coats, jackets, and hats from the fur.

People use the lynx's thick, warm fur to make winter clothing.

There aren't as many lynxes living in the United States as there used to be.

Hunters still trap lynxes in Canada and Alaska. But laws keep them from trapping too many lynxes.

About 200 lynxes live in states other than Alaska. The lynx once lived in 24 states. These days, it lives in only 14 states. People work hard to protect lynxes. They don't want the lynx to die out.

Logging is another danger for lynxes. Loggers are people who cut down trees. They clear away the forests where lynxes live. The lynxes have less land for hunting.

Logging destroys the forests where lynxes live.

A lynx needs to live near the hares and other forest animals that it hunts. And it needs trees for its den. Lynxes do not like to cross open spaces. Open land is not safe. Hunters and other enemies can see and chase lynxes on open land.

Lynxes are safer in the forest than on open land.

When trees are cut down, there is less room for lynxes.

Some loggers clear forests to make room for buildings. People move into the lynx's habitat. They put up houses and businesses.

Roads are a danger for lynxes.

New roads to these buildings break up the lynx's habitat. Lynxes have to cross the roads. Cars and trucks sometimes hit and kill lynxes.

The North American lynx is shy. It likes to live alone. But people keep changing the land where lynxes live. So lynxes will keep hiding. They will move deeper and deeper into the cold, northern forest.

If too many trees are cut down, lynxes will have nowhere to live.

On Sharing a Book

As you know, adults greatly influence a child's attitude toward reading. When a child sees you read, or when you share a book with a child, you're sending a message that reading is important. Show the child that reading a book together is important to you. Find a comfortable, quiet place. Turn off the television and limit other distractions, such as telephone calls.

Be prepared to start slowly. Take turns reading parts of this book. Stop and talk about what you're reading. Talk about the photographs. You may find that much of the shared time is spent discussing just a few pages. This discussion time is valuable for both of you, so don't move through the book too quickly. If the child begins to lose interest, stop reading. Continue sharing the book at another time. When you do pick up the book again, be sure to revisit the parts you have already read. Most importantly, enjoy the book!

Be a Vocabulary Detective

You will find a word list on page 5. Words selected for this list are important to the understanding of the topic of this book. Encourage the child to be a word detective and search for the words as you read the book together. Talk about what the words mean and how they are used in the sentence. Do any of these words have more than one meaning? You will find these words defined in a glossary on page 46.

What about Questions?

Use questions to make sure the child understands the information in this book. Here are some suggestions:

What is this paragraph about? What does this picture show? What do you think we'll learn about next? Could a lynx live in your backyard? Why or why not? What places in a forest are good for a lynx's den? Why is the lynx such a good hunter? How does a lynx survive during cold winters? What do you think it's like to be a lynx? What is your favorite part of the book? Why?

If the child has questions, don't hesitate to respond with questions of your own, such as What do *you* think? Why? What is it that you don't know? If the child can't remember certain facts, turn to the index.

Introducing the Index

The index is an important learning tool. It helps readers get information quickly without searching throughout the whole book. Turn to the index on page 47. Choose an entry, such as *kittens*, and ask the child to use the index to find out how lynxes raise their kittens. Repeat this exercise with as many entries as you like. Ask the child to point out the differences between an index and a glossary. (The index helps readers find information quickly, while the glossary tells readers what words mean.)

Where in the World?

Many plants and animals found in the Early Bird Nature Books series live in parts of the world other than the United States. Encourage the child to find the places mentioned in this book on a world map or globe. Take time to talk about climate, terrain, and how you might live in such places.

All the World in Metric!

Although our monetary system is in metric units (based on multiples of 10), the United States is one of the few countries in the world that does not use the metric system of measurement. Here are some conversion activities you and the child can do using a calculator:

WHEN YOU KNOW:	MULTIPLY BY:	TO FIND:
miles	1.609	kilometers
feet	0.3048	meters
inches	2.54	centimeters
gallons	3.785	liters
tons	0.907	metric tons
pounds	0.454	kilograms

Activities

The lynx has excellent hearing. See how good your hearing is. Pretend you are a lynx that is waiting for prey to pass by. Sit outdoors in your backyard or in a park. Be quiet and still. What do you hear? Can you hear animals, such as birds, squirrels, or rabbits, moving?

Make up a story about a lynx. Use the information in this book. Draw or paint pictures to illustrate your story.

Glossary

carnivore (KAHR-nuh-vor): an animal that eats flesh or meat

den: a hidden, safe place for an animal to rest

habitat (HAB-uh-tat): an area where a kind of animal can live and grow

home range: the area where a lynx lives

kittens: baby lynxes

nurse: to drink mother's milk

predator (PREH-duh-tur): an animal that hunts other animals for food

prey: animals that are hunted and eaten by other animals

retracts: pulls back into the paws. A lynx retracts its claws when it isn't using them.

ruff: long fur around a lynx's neck

tufts: the bunches of dark hairs at the tips of a lynx's ears

Index

Pages listed in **bold** type refer to photographs.

About the Authors

Barbara Keevil Parker and Duane F. Parker live and work in Everett, Washington. Ms. Parker is an environmental writer and author. Her books include *North American Wolves, Giraffes,* and *Cheetahs* as well as a book about Susan B. Anthony. The Parkers wrote a book about Miguel D. Cervantes. *Lynxes* is the second book they have written together. Mr. Parker also writes for magazines and journals. The Parkers are members of the Society of Children's Book Writers and Illustrators. Ms. Parker is an instructor at the Institute of Children's Literature.